SMART MONEY

A GUIDE TO FINANCIAL LITERACY FOR CHILDREN

Ephraim Unuigbe

SMART MONEY

A Guide to Financial Literacy for Children

Ephraim Unuigbe

About the book

"Smart Money: A Guide to Financial Literacy for Children" is a comprehensive book designed to help children between the ages of 5 and 15 learn about money and financial management. The book covers a wide range of topics, including earning and saving money, spending and managing money, investing and growing wealth, protecting and insuring assets, and handling financial emergencies.

The book is written in a simple and easy-to-understand style, making it accessible for children of all ages. In addition, it includes interactive exercises and real-life examples to help children apply the concepts they learn to their own lives.

"Smart Money" aims to give children the knowledge and skills they need to make informed financial decisions and build a solid foundation for their financial future. By understanding these concepts and developing good financial habits from a young age, children can set themselves up for success as they grow older.

Ephraim Unuigbe/ Smart Money: A Guide to Financial Literacy for Children

Copyright December 2022 © Ephraim Unuigbe

All rights reserved.

No part of this book may be reproduced, distributed, stored, or transmitted in any form or by any means, including electronic, photocopy, recording, reproducing or resale without the prior written permission of the author and publisher, except in the case of brief quotations embodied in reviews and articles as well as certain other non-commercial uses permitted by copyright law.

Contact the author via info@ephraim-unuigbe.online; ephraim.unuigbe@gmail.com

Dedication

This book is dedicated to my son Daniel Unuigbe

Table of Content

	PAGE
Chapter 1: Introduction to Money	11
Chapter 2: Earning and Saving Money	27
Chapter 3: Spending and Managing Money	40
Chapter 4: Investing and Growing Money	54
Chapter 5: Protecting and Insuring Money	63
Chapter 6: Handling Financial Emergencies	72
Chapter 7: Building Good Financial Habits	79

Preface

Welcome to "Smart Money: A Guide to Financial Literacy for Children"!

As you grow up, you will encounter many financial decisions that will impact your life. Whether it's saving for a college education, buying your first car, or planning for retirement, understanding how to manage your money is a crucial life skill.

This book has been designed to help you build a solid foundation of financial literacy, starting at a young age. We will cover topics such as earning and saving money, spending and managing money, investing and growing wealth, protecting and insuring your assets, and handling financial emergencies. We will also discuss the importance of developing good financial habits and how they can set you up for success in the future.

We hope that this book will be a helpful resource as you learn about the world of money and financial management. By understanding these concepts and developing good financial habits, you can make smart financial decisions that will benefit you in the long run.

Happy reading!

Chapter 1

Introduction to Money

In this chapter, we will explore the basics of money and how it is used in our daily lives.

In the Introduction to Money chapter, children will learn about the basics of money and how it is used in our daily lives. They will learn about the different types of money, such as coins, bills, and debit cards, and the role of banks in managing money and providing financial services.

This chapter will help children understand the importance of money in modern society and how it is used to buy and sell goods and services, as well as how it can be saved and invested in growing wealth over time. Through interactive exercises and real-life examples, children will have the opportunity to apply the concepts they learn to their own lives and begin to develop a foundation of financial literacy.

1.1 What is money, and why do we use it?

Money is a medium of exchange that is used to buy and sell goods and services. It is a way to pay for things without bartering or trading directly. Money makes buying and selling items easier because it has a common value that everyone accepts.

Many types of money are used worldwide, such as coins, bills, and electronic payment methods like debit and credit cards. Money is typically issued and regulated by a government, and its value is based on the level of trust that people have in it.

We use money because it is a convenient and efficient way to exchange value. It allows us to buy and sell things quickly and simplifies the exchange process.

Money also acts as a store of value, meaning that it can be saved and used later.

In addition to its practical uses, money also has a social and psychological role in our lives. For example, it can be a source of security and status and can be used to show appreciation or affection through gifts or charitable donations.

Overall, money is an integral part of our daily lives and plays a central role in the functioning of modern society.

1.2 Different types of money

Many different types of money are used around the world. Some common types, however, money include:

- Coins: Small pieces of metal that are used as money. Coins come in different sizes and denominations and are used for small purchases.

- Bills: Large pieces of paper that are used as money. Bills come in different denominations and are used for larger purchases.

- Debit cards: Cards linked to a bank account can be used to make purchases or withdraw money from an ATM.

- Credit cards: Cards that allow users to borrow money from a lender in order to make purchases. Credit cards must be paid back with interest.

- Electronic money: Money that is stored electronically, such as in a digital wallet or on a prepaid card.

- Cryptocurrencies: Digital currencies that use cryptography for security and are decentralized, meaning they are not regulated by any central authority. Examples include Bitcoin and Ethereum.

- Barter: The direct exchange of goods or services for other goods or services without the use of money.

- Commodity money: Money that is made from a commodity, such as gold or silver, that has value in and of itself.

- Representative money: Money representing a claim on a commodity, such as paper money, that can be exchanged for gold.

- Fiat money: Money that is declared legal tender by a government but has no intrinsic value and is not backed by a commodity. Most modern money is fiat money.

Many other types of money have been used throughout history, and the forms of money used can vary significantly depending on the culture and economic system of a given society.

1.3 The role of banks in managing money

Banks are financial institutions that provide various services, including the safekeeping and managing money. For example, people can deposit their money into a bank account, which is a safe and secure place to keep it. In addition, it offers other financial services, such as loans, investment products, and insurance.

Banks play a variety of roles in the financial system, including:

- Safekeeping and management of money: Banks offer a range of accounts, such as checking and savings accounts, that allow customers to deposit their money in a safe and secure place. Banks also offer various ways to access and manage their money, such as through ATMs, online and mobile banking, and debit cards.

- Lending: Banks lend money to individuals and businesses through loans or credit products. This allows people to borrow money to make large purchases or invest in their businesses. Banks make money by charging interest on the loans they provide.

- Investment products: Banks offer a variety of investment products, such as mutual funds, exchange-traded funds, and individual stocks and bonds, that allow customers to grow their wealth over time. Banks may also offer financial planning and investment advice to help customers make informed decisions about their investments.

- Payment processing: Banks facilitate the transfer of money between individuals and businesses, whether through electronic payments, checks, or wire transfers. They also play a role in processing credit card transactions.

- Insurance: Many banks offer insurance products, such as health insurance, life insurance, and car insurance, to help customers protect their assets and financial well-being.

- Financial education and assistance: Banks may offer financial education resources, such as educational materials and workshops, to help customers understand financial concepts and make informed financial decisions. They may also provide assistance with financial planning, budgeting, and other financial matters.

Overall, banks play a central role in the financial system by providing a range of services that help individuals and businesses manage their money, grow their wealth, and protect their assets.

The Importance of Money In Modern Society

Money plays a vital role in modern society, as it is a medium of exchange that is used to buy and sell goods and services. Without money, it would be difficult to trade and exchange value and the economy would not function as efficiently.

Here are a few other ways in which money is important in modern society:

- Money allows us to purchase the goods and services we need to survive and thrive. It enables us to buy food, clothing, shelter, healthcare, education, and other necessities.

- Money is a store of value. It allows us to save and invest for the future and can be used to plan and achieve our financial goals.

- Money is a way to show appreciation or affection. We can use the money to give gifts or make charitable donations, which can strengthen relationships and contribute to the well-being of others.

- Money is a source of security and status. Having a stable income and financial resources can provide a sense of security and allow us to live a comfortable and fulfilling life.

- Money facilitates economic growth and development. It allows businesses to invest in new technologies, hire employees, and expand their operations, which can drive economic growth and create jobs.

- Money can be used to facilitate trade and increase efficiency. By using money as a medium of exchange, people and businesses can more easily buy and sell goods and services, leading to increased efficiency and productivity.

- Money can be used to improve quality of life. With access to financial resources, people can afford to live in safer and more desirable neighbourhoods, pursue higher education and career opportunities, and enjoy a variety of leisure and cultural activities.

- Money can be used to help people in need. By donating money to charities or supporting social programs, we can help people who are struggling to meet their basic needs and improve their quality of life.

Overall, money plays a central role in modern society and is essential to our daily lives. It allows us to exchange value, plan for the future, and improve our well-being.

Interactive Exercises and Real-Life Examples

Here are a few interactive exercises and real-life examples that could help children apply the concepts they learn about money to their own lives:

- Identify the different types of money: Show children different types of money, such as coins, bills, and debit cards, and have them identify which is which. Then, ask them to give examples of when they might use each type of money.

- Create a budget: Have children create a budget for a week or month, using a list of their anticipated expenses and income. This could include things like allowance, money earned from chores, and money saved from birthdays or holidays. Then, have them think about how they can allocate their money to different categories, such as saving, spending, and giving.

- Play a shopping game: Set up a pretend store with a variety of items for children to "purchase." Give them a set amount of "money" to work with, and have them make decisions about what to buy and how much to spend. This can help them practice making smart spending decisions and understanding the concept of needs vs wants.

- Visit a bank: Take children on a visit to a local bank and observe the different services offered. Ask them questions about what they see and what they think the bank is used for. This can help them understand the role of banks in managing money and providing financial services.

- Discuss real-life examples: Talk with children about real-life examples of how people use money in their daily lives. This could include things like paying for groceries, saving for a family vacation, or investing in a college education. Please encourage them to think about how these decisions might impact their financial well-being.

Chapter 2

Earning and Saving Money

In this chapter, we will explore the ways in which children can earn and save money and the importance of setting financial goals and budgeting for the future.

In this chapter, children will learn about various ways to earn money, such as through allowances, completing tasks or responsibilities around the house, and part-time jobs. They will also learn about the importance of setting financial goals, budgeting and saving money towards those goals.

This chapter will help children understand how to manage their money effectively and plan for their financial future. With interactive exercises and real-life examples, children can apply the concepts they learn to their own lives and develop good financial habits.

2.1 Ways to earn money

There are many different ways that children can earn money, such as:

- Allowance: Many parents give their children an allowance as a way to teach them about money management. Allowances are usually given on a regular basis, such as weekly or monthly, and can be based on the completion of chores or other responsibilities.

- Chores: Children can earn money by completing household chores or tasks for neighbours or family members. This can be an excellent way to learn about the value of hard work and responsibility.

- Part-time jobs: As children get older, they may be able to find part-time jobs, such as babysitting, dog walking, or yard work, to earn extra money. These jobs can teach children the importance of punctuality, reliability, and customer service.

- Selling items: Children can sell items they no longer need or use, such as toys, books, or clothes. They can do this through online marketplaces, garage sales, or by contacting local buyers directly.

- Offering services: Children with certain skills or talents, such as art, music, or sports, may be able to offer their services to others in exchange for money. For example, they could offer to give art lessons, perform at events, or coach sports teams.

- Participating in surveys or focus groups: Children who are at least 13 years old may be able to participate in online surveys or focus groups to earn extra money. These opportunities may be available through market research companies or websites that specialize in paid surveys.

- Renting out items: Children who have items that they are not using, such as sports equipment, musical instruments, or party supplies, may be able to rent them out to others in exchange for money. This can be an excellent way to earn extra money while also decluttering and being environmentally friendly.

- Starting a business: Entrepreneurial-minded Children may be able to start their own business to earn money. This could be something as simple as selling lemonade or baked goods or a more involved business, such as a lawn care or dog walking service.

2.2 Setting financial goals and saving money towards them

Children need to learn about the importance of setting financial goals and saving money towards them. Financial goals could be short-term, such as saving for a new toy or game, or long-term, such as saving for college or a down payment on a house. By setting goals, children can learn about the value of planning and saving for the future.

2.2.1 How to Set financial Goals and save money towards them

To help children set financial goals and save money towards them, you can try the following steps:

- Discuss the importance of saving money: Talk with children about the importance of saving money for the future. Explain that saving can help them achieve their goals, such as buying a new bike or saving for college, and that it is an excellent habit to develop.

- Encourage children to think about their goals: Ask children to think about what they would like to save money for. For example, they may have short-term goals, such as saving for a new toy or game, or long-term goals, such as saving for a down payment on a house. Encourage them to be specific and consider what they will need to do to achieve their goals.

- Help children create a plan: Once children have identified their goals, help them create a plan for saving money towards them. This could include setting aside a certain amount of money from each allowance or part-time job or finding ways to earn extra money through chores or other activities.

- Encourage children to track their progress: Help children track their progress towards their financial goals by creating a chart or spreadsheet. This can help them see how much they have saved and how close they are to achieving their goals.

- Celebrate achievements: When children reach their financial goals, celebrate their achievements and encourage them to set new goals. This can help them continue to develop good financial habits and become more financially responsible over time.

Overall, by setting financial goals and saving money towards them, children can learn about the importance of planning and saving for the future and develop good financial habits that will serve them well in adulthood.

2.3 The importance of budgeting and saving for the future

Budgeting is the process of managing money by allocating it towards different expenses and goals. It can help children understand how much money they have and how to make the most of it.

By budgeting, children can learn how to allocate their money towards their most important priorities and make the most of their financial resources. It can also help them avoid overspending and debt and ensure that they have enough money set aside for emergencies or unexpected expenses. Budgeting and saving for the future can help children build financial stability and security and prepare for their long-term financial goals."

There are many benefits to budgeting and saving for the future, including the following:

- Increased financial stability: By budgeting and saving money, children can build a financial foundation that will help them achieve their financial goals and improve their overall financial well-being.
- Better money management skills: Budgeting requires children to think about their spending and saving habits, which can help them develop good money management skills and make more informed financial decisions.

- Greater financial independence: By learning how to budget and save money, children can become more financially independent and capable of managing their own finances as they grow older.

- Preparation for future expenses: Budgeting and saving can help children prepare for future expenses, such as education, housing, and retirement, by building a financial cushion that they can draw on when needed.

Interactive Exercises and Real-Life Examples

Here are a few interactive exercises and real-life examples that could help children apply the concepts they learn about earning and saving money to their own lives:

- Create a chore chart: Help children create a chore chart that lists the tasks they are responsible for completing and the amount of money they will earn for each task. Please encourage them to set aside a certain amount of their earnings for saving and budget the rest for spending or giving.

- Play a money-earning game: Create a game in which children have to complete tasks or challenges in order to earn money. This could include things like solving math problems, completing puzzles, or answering trivia questions. Then, have them keep track of their earnings and decide how they want to allocate their money towards different goals or expenses.

- Discuss real-life earning and saving scenarios: Talk with children about real-life scenarios in which people earn and save money, such as starting a business, saving for a down payment on a house, or investing in a retirement account. Please encourage them to think about the financial goals and challenges these people face and how they work towards them.

- Visit a bank or credit union: Take children on a visit to a local bank or credit union and have them observe the different services that are offered. Ask them how people earn and save money and how banks and credit unions help them achieve their financial goals.

- Set financial goals and track progress: Help children set financial goals and create a plan for saving money towards

Chapter 3

Spending and Managing Money

This chapter will explore the importance of making wise spending decisions and understanding the concept of needs vs wants. We will also discuss the use of credit cards and loans and the role they play in managing money.

In this chapter, children will learn the importance of making wise spending decisions, understanding the concept of needs vs wants, and the role of credit cards and loans in managing money. In addition, they will learn about the potential risks and costs associated with using credit and the importance of paying bills on time and avoiding debt.

This chapter will teach children how to make informed financial decisions and manage their money effectively. Then, through interactive exercises and real-life examples, children can apply the concepts they learn to their own lives and develop good financial habits.

3.1 Making intelligent spending decisions

Children must learn to make wise spending decisions to manage their money effectively. Making intelligent spending decisions can include comparing prices, shopping for the best deals, and avoiding impulse purchases.

Here are a few tips for children to help them make intelligent spending decisions:

- Compare prices: Encourage children to shop and compare prices from different retailers or online sites before purchasing. Comparing prices can help them ensure they get the best value for their money.

- Think about needs vs wants: Help children distinguish between needs and wants and encourage them to prioritize their needs when making spending decisions. Understanding the difference can help them avoid overspending on unnecessary items.

- Set a budget: Help children create a budget that outlines how much money they have to spend and how they want to allocate it towards different goals or expenses. Setting a budget can help them make more informed spending decisions and stay on track with their financial goals.

- Avoid impulse purchases: Encourage children to think carefully before making a purchase and avoid impulse buying. Remind them that they can take time to consider their options and do research before making a decision.

- Use cash or debit cards: To avoid overspending, encourage children to use cash or debit cards instead of credit cards whenever possible. Learning the proper use of cash or credit card can help them stay within their budget and avoid accruing credit card debt.

There are many important reasons why children need to learn how to make wise spending decisions. Here are a few examples:

- Avoiding overspending: Making smart spending decisions can help children avoid overspending and falling into debt. In addition, they can ensure they get the best value for their money by carefully considering their purchases and comparing prices.

- Staying on a budget: By making wise spending decisions, children can stay on budget and make the most of their financial resources. Staying on a budget can help them achieve their financial goals and avoid financial difficulties.

- Building good financial habits: Making smart spending decisions is vital to develop, as it can set the foundation for sound financial management skills in adulthood.

- Improving financial well-being: Children can improve their overall economic well-being and increase their financial stability and security by making wise spending decisions.

3.2 Understanding the concept of needs vs wants

Another important concept for children to understand is the difference between needs and wants. Needs such as food, clothing, and shelter are necessary for survival. Wants are things we would like to have but are optional. Teaching children to distinguish between needs and wants can help them make more informed spending decisions and avoid overspending.

Here is a table that illustrates the concept of needs vs wants:

Needs	Wants
Food	Toys
Clothing	Electronics
Shelter	Luxury items
Healthcare	Entertainment
Transportation	Clothes

In this table, the items in the "Needs" column are essential for survival, such as food, clothing, and shelter. The items in the "Wants" column are things we would like to have but are not essential. Teaching children to distinguish between their needs and wants can help them make more informed spending decisions and avoid overspending.

3.3 The use of credit cards and loans

Credit cards and loans are financial products that allow people to borrow money and make purchases on credit. While they can be helpful in certain situations, children need to understand the potential risks and costs associated with using credit. This includes understanding interest rates, fees, and the importance of paying bills on time.

There are several potential risks and costs associated with using credit, including:

- Interest: When you borrow money on credit, you are typically required to pay interest on the amount you borrow. Interest is a fee that the lender charges to use their money. Therefore, the higher the interest rate, the more you will have to pay in total.

- Fees: Credit cards and loans may also have fees, such as annual fees, late payment fees, or balance transfer fees. These fees can add up and significantly increase the overall cost of borrowing.

- Debt: If you use credit and cannot pay off your balance in full each month, you may accrue debt. This can be a burden, as you will be required to pay interest on the amount you owe, making it more challenging to pay off your balance.

- Credit score: Your credit score is a measure of your creditworthiness and is based on your credit history. If you use credit responsibly and pay your bills on time, you can build a good credit score. However, if you misuse credit or make late payments, it can damage your credit score and make it more difficult to obtain loans or credit cards in the future.

- Overdraft fees: If you have a checking account and use a debit card or checks to make purchases, you may be at risk of overdrafting if you do not have enough money in your account to cover the transaction. If this happens, you may be charged an overdraft fee.

- Fraud: Credit card fraud is when someone uses your credit card without your permission to make unauthorized purchases. This can be a risk if you lose your credit card or if it is stolen. To protect against credit card fraud, it is important to keep your credit card information secure and report any suspicious activity to your credit card issuer.

- Identity theft: Identity theft is when someone uses your personal information, such as your name, address, or social security number, to open credit accounts or make purchases in your name. To protect against identity theft, it is important to keep your personal information secure and to regularly check your credit reports to ensure that there are no unauthorized accounts or activity.

These are just a few examples of the potential risks and costs associated with using credit. It is important for children to be aware of these risks and to take steps to protect themselves and their financial well-being. Overall, children need to understand the potential risks and costs associated with using credit and with using credit responsibly in order to avoid financial difficulties.

Interactive exercises and real-life examples

Here are a few interactive exercises and real-life examples that could help children apply the concepts they learn about spending and managing money to their own lives:

- Create a shopping list: Help children create a shopping list and encourage them to compare prices and look for deals. Then, have them consider their budget and ensure they are only purchasing items they need.

- Play a money management game: Create a game in which children have to make spending decisions within a budget. For example, you could give them a set amount of money and have them decide how to allocate it towards different expenses, such as rent, groceries, and entertainment.

- Discuss real-life credit scenarios: Talk with children about real-life scenarios in which people use credit, such as buying a car or taking out a mortgage. Please encourage them to think about the risks and costs associated with using credit and how to use credit responsibly.

- Use a credit card simulation: Use a credit card simulation tool or game to help children understand how credit cards work and the potential risks and costs associated with using them.

- Set financial goals and track progress: Help children set financial goals, such as saving for a big purchase or paying off a credit card balance, and create a plan for achieving them. Please encourage them to track their progress and make adjustments to their spending and saving habits as needed.

Chapter 4

Investing and Growing Money

In this chapter, children will learn about the basics of investing and how it can help grow wealth over time. They will also learn about different types of investment options, such as stocks, mutual funds, and real estate, and the importance of diversification and managing risk.

4.1 The basics of investing

Investing is the act of putting money into financial instruments or assets with the goal of earning a return. There are many different types of investments, including stocks, bonds, mutual funds, and real estate, each with its own risks and potential returns. By investing their money, children can earn a higher return than they would by simply saving it in a bank account.

4.2 Different types of investment options

There are many different types of investment options available, each with its own risks and potential returns. Some common types of investments include:

- Stocks: Stocks represent ownership in a company and can be bought and sold on the stock market. The value of a stock can go up or down based on the performance of the company and market conditions.

- Mutual funds: A mutual fund is a type of investment that pools together money from many investors and uses it to buy a diversified portfolio of stocks, bonds, or other securities. Mutual funds offer professional management and diversification but also come with fees and risks.

- Real estate: Real estate investment involves buying, holding, and potentially selling property for a profit. Real estate can be a long-term investment and can be subject to market fluctuations and other risks.

4.3 The importance of diversification and managing risk

Diversification is the practice of spreading investments across different asset classes and types of investments in order to reduce risk. By diversifying their investments, children can reduce the overall risk of their portfolio and increase their chances of earning a positive return.

It is also important for children to understand the risks associated with different types of investments and to manage their risks accordingly. This may involve avoiding investments that are too risky for their financial goals or risk tolerance or using tools like stop-loss orders to limit potential losses.

Importance of Diversification and Managing Risk

Diversification and risk management are important concepts in investing, as they can help reduce the overall risk of an investment portfolio and increase the chances of earning a positive return. Here are a few reasons why diversification and risk management are important:

- Reduce risk: By diversifying investments across different asset classes and types of investments, investors can potentially reduce the overall risk of their portfolio. This is because different types of investments may perform differently in different market conditions, so spreading investments across multiple types can help reduce the impact of any one investment underperforming.

- Increase chances of earning a positive return: By diversifying and managing risk, investors can potentially increase their chances of earning a positive return on their investments. This is because they are not relying on any one investment to perform well but rather a diversified portfolio that is better equipped to withstand market fluctuations.

- Achieve financial goals: By diversifying and managing risk, investors can help ensure that their investments are aligned with their financial goals. For example, if their goal is to save for retirement, they may choose a more conservative investment strategy with a lower level of risk in order to protect their savings.

By understanding these concepts, children can develop good financial habits and make more informed investment decisions.

Overall, this chapter will teach children about the basics of investing and how it can help them grow wealth over time. They will learn about different types of investment options and the importance of diversification and risk management in investing. Then, through interactive exercises and real-life examples, children will have the opportunity to apply the concepts they learn to their own lives and develop good financial habits.

Interactive Exercises and Real-Life Examples

Here are a few interactive exercises and real-life examples that could help children apply the concepts they learn about investing and growing money to their own lives:

- Invest in a mock portfolio: Set up a mock portfolio for children to practice investing in different types of investments. For example, you could use a simulation tool or game or create a pretend portfolio using fake money.

- Research different investment options: Encourage children to research various types of investment options, such as stocks, mutual funds, and real estate, and compare their potential risks and returns.

- Discuss real-life investment scenarios: Talk with children about real-life investment scenarios, such as saving for retirement or buying a rental property. Please encourage them to think about the risks and potential returns of different investment options and how to create a diversified portfolio.

- Create a budget and savings plan: Help children create a budget and savings plan that includes a portion of their money for investing. Please encourage them to set financial goals and allocate their investments towards those goals.

- Monitor and review investments: Have children monitor and review their investments regularly to see how they perform and make any necessary adjustments to their portfolio.

Chapter 5

Protecting and Insuring Money

In this chapter, children will learn about the importance of protecting assets through insurance, such as health, car, and home insurance. They will also learn about the risks and benefits of different insurance policies and how to choose the right coverage for their needs. This chapter will teach children the skills they need to make informed insurance decisions and protect their assets and financial well-being. Through interactive exercises and real-life examples, children will have the opportunity to apply the concepts they learn to their own lives and develop good financial habits.

5.1 The importance of protecting assets through insurance

Insurance is a way to protect assets, such as your health, car, or home, against unexpected risks or losses. By paying a regular premium, you can transfer the risk of potential losses to an insurance company, which agrees to compensate you for any covered losses. As a result, insurance can provide financial protection and peace of mind and is an important consideration when managing your money.

There are many different types of insurance policies that children should be aware of, depending on their needs and assets. Here are a few examples:

- Health insurance: Health insurance is a type of insurance that covers medical expenses, such as hospital stays, doctor visits, and prescription medications. Health insurance can help protect against the high costs of medical care and is an important consideration for children and their families.

- Car insurance: Car insurance is a type of insurance that covers damages to a car or injuries sustained in a car accident. It is typically required by law and can help protect against the costs of repairing or replacing a car or covering medical expenses.

- Home Insurance: Home insurance is a type of insurance that covers damages to a home, such as from a fire or natural disaster, and personal property, such as furniture and appliances. It can also provide liability coverage if someone is injured on the property. Home insurance is an important consideration for homeowners and renters.

- Life insurance: Life insurance is a type of insurance that provides financial protection for loved ones in the event of the policyholder's death. It can be used to cover funeral expenses and outstanding debts or provide ongoing financial support for dependents.

These are just a few examples of the different insurance policies that children should be aware of. It is important for children to understand their own insurance needs and choose coverage appropriate for their assets and financial goals.

5.2 Understanding the risks and benefits of different insurance policies

Many different types of insurance policies are available, each with its own risks and benefits. Children need to understand the risks and benefits of other insurance policies in order to choose the right coverage for their needs. Some things to consider when selecting insurance coverage include the following:

- The type of coverage: Different insurance policies offer different types of coverage, such as liability coverage, property coverage, or personal injury coverage. It is important to choose the coverage that is appropriate for your needs and assets.

- The cost of premiums: Insurance premiums are the regular payments made to an insurance company in exchange for coverage. Premiums can vary based on the type of insurance and the level of coverage. Therefore, it is important to compare premiums and choose a policy that is affordable and provides adequate coverage.

- The exclusions and limitations: Insurance policies typically have exclusions and limitations, which are circumstances in which the policy does not provide coverage. It is important to understand these exclusions and limitations so you know what is and is not covered by your policy.

Overall, this chapter will teach children the importance of protecting assets through insurance and the risks and benefits of different insurance policies. Then, through interactive exercises and real-life examples, children will have the opportunity to apply the concepts they learn to their own lives and develop good financial habits.

Interactive Exercises and Real-Life Examples

Here are a few interactive exercises and real-life examples that could help children apply the concepts they learn about protecting and insuring money in their own lives:

- Research different insurance options: Encourage children to research different insurance options, such as health, car, and home insurance, and compare their risks and benefits.

- Create a budget and insurance plan: Help children create a budget that includes insurance premiums and encourage them to set financial goals for their insurance coverage.

- Discuss real-life insurance scenarios: Talk with children about real-life insurance scenarios, such as getting into a car accident or experiencing a natural disaster. Please encourage them to consider the importance of adequate insurance coverage in these situations.

- Use an insurance simulation tool: Use an insurance simulation tool or game to help children understand the risks and benefits of different insurance policies and how to choose the right coverage for their needs.

- Review insurance coverage: Encourage children to review their insurance coverage regularly to ensure it is still appropriate for their needs and assets.

Chapter 6

Handling Financial Emergencies

In this chapter, children will learn the importance of planning for unexpected expenses and financial emergencies. They will also learn about the role of emergency savings and how to build them up.

Overall, this chapter will teach children the importance of planning for unexpected expenses and financial emergencies and the role of emergency savings in protecting their economic well-being. Through interactive exercises and real-life examples, children will have the opportunity to apply the concepts they learn to their own lives and develop good financial habits.

6.1 Planning for unexpected expenses and financial emergencies

Unexpected expenses and financial emergencies can happen to anyone, and it is important to be prepared for them. This may involve setting aside money in an emergency fund or having insurance coverage to protect against certain types of losses. By planning for unexpected expenses and financial emergencies, children can help protect their financial well-being and peace of mind.

6.2 The role of emergency savings and how to build them up

An emergency fund is a savings account expressly set aside for unexpected expenses and financial emergencies. It is important to have an emergency fund because it can provide a financial cushion to help cover unexpected expenses without having to borrow money or charge them to a credit card. To build up an emergency fund, children can:

- Set a savings goal: Determine how much money you want to save in your emergency fund and create a plan for reaching that goal.

- Set aside a portion of your income: Determine how much money you can realistically save each month and set aside a portion of your income for your emergency fund.

- Find ways to save money: Look for ways to save money, such as by cutting expenses or finding additional sources of income, and use the extra money to contribute to your emergency fund.

- Keep emergency savings separate: It is important to keep them separate from your other savings and investments, so you are not tempted to spend them on non-emergency expenses.

Interactive Exercises and Real-Life Examples

Here are a few interactive exercises and real-life examples that could help children apply the concepts they learn about handling financial emergencies to their own lives:

- Create a budget and emergency fund plan: Help children create a budget that includes a plan for building an emergency fund. Encourage them to set a savings goal and determine how much money they can realistically save each month.

- Research different savings options: Encourage children to research other savings options, such as savings and money market accounts, and compare their risks and returns.

- Discuss real-life financial emergencies: Talk with children about real-life financial emergencies, such as a car breaking down or a medical expense, and how an emergency fund can help cover these expenses.

- Use a savings simulation tool: Use a savings simulation tool or game to help children understand the importance of building up an emergency fund and how to save money effectively.

- Review and adjust emergency savings: Encourage children to review their emergency savings regularly and make any necessary adjustments to their plan to ensure they are on track to reach their savings goals.

Chapter 7

Building Good Financial Habits

In this chapter, children will learn about the importance of developing good financial habits from a young age. They will also learn about tips for building a solid financial foundation for the future.

Overall, this chapter will teach children about the importance of developing good financial habits from a young age and provide tips for building a solid financial foundation for the future. Through interactive exercises and real-life examples, children will have the opportunity to apply the concepts they learn to their own lives and develop good financial habits.

7.1 The importance of developing good financial habits from a young age

Creating good financial habits from a young age can set children up for success in the future. Sound financial practices include things like saving money, budgeting, and making informed financial decisions. By developing these habits early on, children can build a solid financial foundation that will serve them well throughout their lives.

7.2 Tips for building a solid financial foundation for the future

Here are a few tips for children to consider as they work towards building a solid financial foundation for the future:

- Start saving early: The earlier children save, the more time their money has to grow and compound. Encourage children to set aside a portion of their income for saving and investing and to set financial goals for their savings.

- Learn about financial concepts: Encourage children to learn about financial concepts, such as budgeting, investing, and insurance, and how they can apply these concepts to their own lives.

- Make informed financial decisions: Help children develop the skills they need to make informed financial decisions, such as comparing prices, understanding the risks and benefits of different financial products, and protecting their assets through insurance.

- Seek financial advice: Encourage children to seek financial advice from trusted sources, such as financial advisors or financial education resources, when making important financial decisions.

- Create a financial plan: Help children create a financial plan that includes goals for saving, investing, and spending and a budget to help them stay on track.

- Protect your credit: Encourage children to protect their credit by paying their bills on time, managing their debt wisely, and monitoring their credit reports for errors.

- Be proactive about your financial well-being: Encourage children to be proactive about their financial well-being by staying informed about their finances, seeking financial advice when needed, and taking control of their financial future.

- Create a budget and stick to it: It can help children understand how much money they have and how to make the most of it. Encourage children to track their income and expenses, set financial goals, and make adjustments as needed to stay on track.

- Learn to manage debt: It is important for children to understand the role of debt in their financial lives and how to manage it responsibly. Encourage children to avoid unnecessary debt, make timely payments, and understand the terms and conditions of any obligations they take on.

- Save for the long-term: Encourage children to save for the long-term by setting financial goals and investing their savings in a diversified portfolio. This can help them build wealth over time and prepare for the future.

- Protect your assets: Encourage children to protect their assets through insurance and other risk management strategies, such as creating an emergency fund or maintaining proper maintenance on their possessions.

Interactive exercises and real-life examples

Here are a few interactive exercises and real-life examples that could help children apply the concepts they learn about building good financial habits to their own lives:

- Create a budget: Encourage children to create a budget that includes their income, expenses, and financial goals. Then, help them track their spending and make adjustments as needed to stay on track.

- Set financial goals and create a plan: Encourage children to set financial goals, such as saving for college or a down payment on a house and create a plan for reaching those goals.

- Learn about financial concepts: Encourage children to learn about financial concepts, such as budgeting, investing, and insurance, and how they can apply these concepts to their own lives.

- Use financial education resources: Encourage children to use financial education resources, such as online courses, videos, or games, to learn about financial concepts and develop good financial habits.

- Seek professional advice: Encourage children to seek professional financial advice from trusted sources, such as financial advisors or financial education resources, when making important financial decisions.

- Overall, these interactive exercises and real-life examples can help children apply the concepts they learn about building good financial habits to their own lives and develop good financial habits.

Acknowledgement

To my dearest companion and guide, the Holy Spirit, who has always been my counsellor, helper, intercessor, advocate, strengthener, and standby. Thank you for your constant presence and support

About The Author

Ephraim Unuigbe holds several credentials, including a BSc in Accounting and membership in the Institute of Chartered Accountants of Nigeria. He is also a Certified Information Systems Auditor, certified by the Information Systems Audit and Control Association. In addition to his background in accounting, Unuigbe is also a certified public speaker and career personal finance coach.

Ephraim is currently employed at one of the leading accounting firms in the United Kingdom, where he is responsible for providing assurance services to corporate clients. In addition to his professional pursuits, Ephraim is also actively involved in the community. He serves as the Director of Corporate Governance on the board of HACTRI, a Nigerian literacy organization. He is a board member of Itchen Sixth Form College in the United Kingdom.

Ephraim is married to Marian Unuigbe and has two children, Eseohen Elizabeth and Daniel Chukwudi.

Other Books by The Author to Date

1. Succeeding in your career - A Roadmap for Graduates & Young Professionals

2. Let's talk about money - A guide to Personal Finances for Young Adults

3. How to choose a career path - A Spiritual Perspective to Career Choice & Life

4. Managing Family Finance - for Career Couples

5. Career & Romance - How to Find Your Soul Mate as a Single Career Professional

6. The Career Woman's Guide to SINGLE PARENTING: For Single Female Career Professionals with teenage kids between the ages of 12 -19.

7. Understanding investment for beginners

8. Understanding accounting for the non-accountant

9. The Essential Handbook for Starting a Food, Flower, Retail, Coffee Shop Business

10. How to be a good person for Children

All available on amazon.com and www.ephraim-unuigbe.online

Contact the author via info@ephraim-unuigbe.online or ephraim.unuigbe@gmail.com

Services We Offer

Career Counselling

We assist individuals of all ages in clarifying and attaining their career goals. We also teach students the development of learner-centred skills they can utilise in their academic careers and life beyond.

Personal Finance Coaching

Personal finance refers to how well people adhere to a budget when managing their finances. Over time, the goal is to save money while also spending money on needed resources and allocating a particular amount for each living expense. With my guidance, you will learn how to make, manage, and multiply your money.

CV Review and Writing

The modern world of employment demands that your CV stands out, and we provide a range of services through which our professional CV writers can create the CV just for you. Every CV we create is tailored specifically to meet your needs.

Cover Letter and Personal Statement

We will provide you with a professional who can write you a high-performing letter for your job application or personal statement. Paired with our professionally written CV, you can differentiate yourself from other applicants.

LinkedIn Profile Optimization

You can take your LinkedIn profile to the next level and turn it into a powerful career tool that highlights your abilities and experiences and impresses your contacts.

Interview Coaching

Our professionals help you be the best candidate your potential employer has ever seen. A well-rounded approach that addresses the verbal and non-verbal factors.

www.ingramcontent.com/pod-product-compliance
Lightning Source LLC
Chambersburg PA
CBHW070257220526
45465CB00004B/1646